Maison Rouge

MEMORIES OF A CHILDHOOD IN WAR

Liliane Leila Juma

Maison Rouge

MEMORIES OF A CHILDHOOD IN WAR

Liliane Leila Juma

Tradewind Books
VANCOUVER • LONDON

Published in USA and the UK in 2020

Text © 2019 Liliane Leila Juma
Cover art © 2019 François Cauvin
Map by Jeffrey L. Ward
Cover & book design by Jacqueline Wang

The paper is 100% post-consumer recycled and processed chlorine- and acid-free.

Printed in Canada

2 4 6 8 10 9 7 5 3 1

Cataloguing-in-Publication Data for this book
is available from The British Library.

Library and Archives Canada Cataloguing in Publication

Title: Maison Rouge : memories of a childhood in war / Liliane Leila Juma.
Names: Juma, Liliane Leila, 1982- author.
Identifiers: Canadiana (print) 20190210796 | Canadiana (ebook) 20190210834 |
ISBN 9781926890302 (softcover) | ISBN 9781926890364 (EPUB)
Subjects: LCSH: Juma, Liliane Leila, 1982-—Juvenile literature. | LCSH: Juma,
Liliane Leila, 1982-—
Childhood and youth—Juvenile literature. | LCSH: Congo (Democratic
Republic)—History—1997-—
Juvenile literature. | LCSH: Congo (Democratic Republic)—Social conditions—
21st century—Juvenile literature. | LCSH: Refugees—Congo (Democratic
Republic)—Biography—Juvenile literature. | LCSH: Refugees—Canada—
Biography—Juvenile literature.
Classification: LCC DT658.2.J86 A3 2019 | DDC j967.5103/3092—dc23

The publisher thanks the Government of Canada, the Canada Council
for the Arts and Livres Canada Books for their financial support.
We also thank the Government of the Province of British Columbia
for the financial support we have received through
the Book Publishing Tax Credit program
and the British Columbia Arts Council.

Canada Council   Conseil des Arts
for the Arts   du Canada

BRITISH COLUMBIA
ARTS COUNCIL
Supported by the Province of British Columbia

Canada

LIVRES CANADA BOOKS

Dedication

To my beautiful Maman, Lina Iza Leonie Chikwerere Biraheka Zubeda.

To my beloved Papa, Mzee Juma Omari, may Allah have mercy on your soul, and may you rest in peace.

To my beautiful sisters, Farida Juma and Shany Juma.

Our life journey as refugees was a time of great struggle for our family, and I am determined to come to the aid of other girls and women to the best of my ability.

Author's Note

Leolina was my childhood nickname, so I use it in the book to tell my story. Lela was the name given to me by my father. Leila is how my French school spelled Lela. Liliane was my middle name. When I became a refugee, the Government of Canada put the name Liliane Juma on my ID card. So that became my official name, instead of my real name, Leila Liliane Juma.

That kind of thing happens to immigrants—especially refugees.

Introduction

D.R. Congo: An Overview

The Democratic Republic of Congo (DRC) has experienced the deadliest war in the world since World War Two. An estimated six million Congolese perished between 1996 and 2007 as a result of two Congo wars. Half of the victims of the war were children under the age of five. Women have also paid a terrible price with hundreds of thousands of women being raped as a war strategy. The conflict is a product of two invasions led primarily by Congo's neighbours Rwanda and Uganda, first in 1996 and again in 1998. The initial rationale for the invasion was the pursuit of rebel militias who perpetrated the 1994 genocide in Rwanda, however, it quickly became evident that Congo's neighbours were intent on plundering Congo of its riches.

Congo is endowed with precious and strategic minerals such as gold, diamonds, copper, tin, coltan and a host of other natural resources worth an estimated $24 trillion. Congo's riches have long attracted major global corporations in pursuit of minerals that are vital to the technology, electronics, automobile, aerospace and military industries. Two key minerals that directly tie consumers to the Congo are coltan, which is needed for cell phones, and cobalt, which is vital to the functioning of electric modes of transport.

Congo is home to the largest United Nations peacekeeping force in the world with an estimated 18,000 peacekeepers. However, there are still several dozen militia groups operating in the east of the country rendering large swaths of eastern Congo unstable and insecure. Recent elections in the Congo held high expectations of stabilizing the country. In a country with a median age of 17 years old, Congolese youth are determined to take the lead in transforming their country from a conflict-ridden nation to one of peace, stability and prosperity.

Kambale Musavuli
Spokesperson, Friends of the Congo
Washington, DC

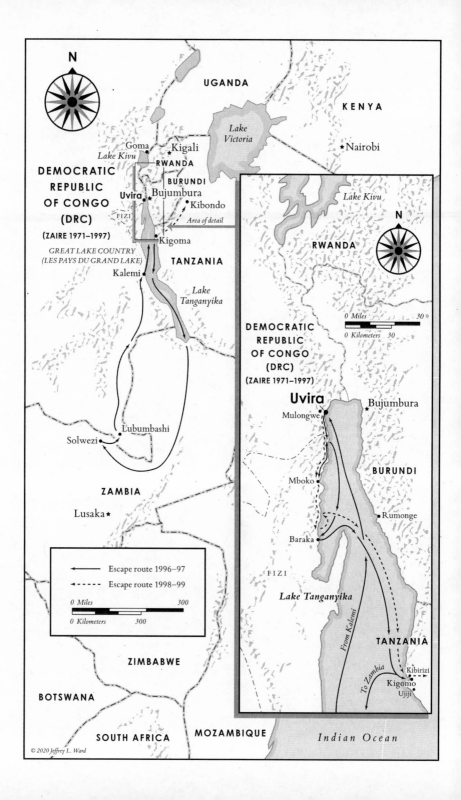

Journey's End

Rain pounded on the roof of the leaky tent, and small puddles were forming at our feet. The smiling UN official held out his hand. "Welcome, madame," he said in Swahili. "Welcome to Tanzania."

Maman smiled and shook his hand. "My name is Leonie Cibibi, the wife of Omar Juma, from Congo."

He sat down at a long desk piled high with folders and wrote the name down in a big book. "Welcome, Leonie. And Mr Omar?"

Maman looked down. "He was taken away."

"I'm so sorry," the UN official said.

Maman gestured to me. "This is my daughter, Leolina. She is sixteen."

"Welcome, Leolina." He wrote down my name.

"And these are my other daughters, Fifi, Mimi and Massy."

My little sisters bobbed their heads.

"Welcome Fifi, Mimi and Massy. And this young man?"

"He is my brother, Rajab," I said. "We call him Raja."

"My name is Rajab too," the official said, grinning. He patted Raja's head. "That makes us brothers, you and I."

Raja pointed to the baby. "This is little Moise."

The officer wrote the names down. "Where are you from in Congo?"

Maman replied, "From Uvira near the border of Burundi and Rwanda at the very top of Lake Tanganyika."

"There are many others here from your city," he said, ushering us outside. "Let me show you where you'll stay until you find permanent refuge."

He led us into the pouring rain. "Hurry, madame. Hurry, children." He guided us to a small mud hut. "I have to leave you now. If you need anything, just find me and I'll try to help."

We gave thanks to Allah for saving our family from a horrific fate, one that had taken the lives of many many thousands of innocent men and woman, boys and girls—a terrible fate that was indifferent to nationality or ethnicity, religion or politics, wealth or poverty or education.

Maison Rouge

Blessed with the love and support of family, friends and neighbours, my life before the wars had been happy and carefree.

Before the Congo wars came to Uvira, before Yayabo and the militias moved in, before my father was taken away—I was living happily with my parents, my brother and sisters, and Sarafina, our nanny and housekeeper, in our home, Maison Rouge, close to the shore of Lake Tanganyika.

My married sister, Furaha, a French teacher, lived in nearby Burundi, and another older sister, Aza, lived there too. An older brother, Abdoul, lived in Rwanda.

Uvira lay in the lush Rift Valley with green mountains looming in the horizon above the town. There were fruit trees and palm trees everywhere—mango, coconut, pomegranate, date, pomade, avocado, orange, lemon and fig.

Almost every house in the town had at least one fruit or palm tree in its garden, plus a small plot with beans, vegetables and flowers.

When I was little, I had planted a tree in our garden that produced both oranges and lemons. In the back corner of the garden, there were flowers, sugarcane and tomatoes. There were birds too—so many kinds and so many colours— the brilliant peafowl, our national bird, also quetzals, hoopoes, hornbills, kingfishers and hundreds more.

Maison Rouge, the house itself, had five bedrooms and three large living rooms. Its outside walls were red and the inside flooring was also red. My bedroom, however, had three pink walls and one purple wall.

Our household included people my mother and father helped, and those who worked with us as housekeepers, cooks, tutors, nannies and seamstresses.

A very old woman named Bibi, which means

grandmother in Swahili, also lived with us. She was a refugee from Burundi with no family and must have been about 100 years old. We took care of her, and Maman had given her a suite in the garden.

At Maison Rouge, after I woke up in the morning, I would walk down three stairs into our large garden, breathing in the *fajir*—the early morning air. Then I would sit under the orange tree and wash, pouring water onto my hands and feet from a silver vase called *birika* in Swahili. This ritual is called *wudu*, meaning ablutions—the ritual morning cleansing that Muslims do.

Returning to my bedroom, I had to walk between the outbuildings my father had built for our large extended family and people who didn't have a place to stay. There were also a couple of work spaces, one for Papa's theatre and musical groups, and one for Maman's studio, where she designed clothes and held women's meetings.

Our garden was used for family gatherings

and big celebrations. I remember well the last one we hosted at Maison Rouge before the wars came. It was the *Eid*, at the end of *Ramadan*, and Papa and Maman had invited all our neighbours, including Christians, to join us.

Everyone loved our Baswahili food, a mixture of traditional Congolese, Indian and Arab dishes. Local people also used the word Baswahili as a nickname for Muslims who speak Swahili.

I made pilau, a chicken and rice dish garnished with savoury spices, and curried vegetables and *chapatis*. Papa made deep-fried *beignets*, cream-filled croissants and sweet cakes. Maman put together big plates of nuts and fruit. Our housekeeper, Sarafina, squeezed hundreds of oranges into enough juice to fill many many tumblers.

Maman loved to help people, especially women in need. As well as having offered Bibi a home at Maison Rouge, she had given her money to start her own business making chapatis and roti.

Our family friend, Safi, was a good storyteller and loved to chat. So Maman opened a small food store where Safi could sit and enjoy talking to people. Women would take merchandise on loan and sell it in the market at retail for a profit. Often in the evenings, I would help Safi with her reading and writing.

Apart from that business, Maman also had a salon for women and a restaurant that I helped manage during the summer break. Most of my friends, girls and boys, worked with me, and we gave them small salaries so that they could save to buy their uniforms and school supplies.

While we were much better off than our neighbours, my father taught me to appreciate our good fortune and be humble. We cared for and supported strangers in need, making them part of our family and giving them hope to rebuild their lives, whether they had suffered from war, or had simply been rejected by family.

Papa was highly respected in Uvira. People

would say, "Juma Omar is such a kindly and generous man."

"Whatever we have," Papa would say, "we need to share with others. We came to this world empty-handed and will leave empty-handed. Only our good deeds will outlive us. That's what we will be remembered for."

I adored Papa so much, and never imagined that one day a time would come when I would be separated from him forever.

My School

My school, the Mwanga Institute, was a Catholic elementary and secondary school. The Catholic kids would say a prayer at assembly, first making the sign of the cross and then reciting the "Our Father" prayer. As a Muslim, I would pray silently, respecting others' prayers and religions. There were many Muslim children at the school and kids from various ethnic backgrounds—Tutsis from the Congo, Rwanda and Burundi, and Hutus from all three countries as well. There were also Belgian kids, whose parents had stayed on in the Congo after independence, and Indian and Pakistani kids, whose parents had fled the violence after partition of the subcontinent.

One day when my friends and I were walking home from school, we stopped to talk by a baobab tree. Out of the blue, one of the girls, Saga, asked, "Because Zaina is shorter than me, does that mean she is Hutu?"

"What nonsense," Zaina said.

"Why do you say that?" I asked.

"I'm Tutsi," Zaina said, "but I had to flee here alone, without my family, because I am short and look Hutu. In Burundi, some innocent people have been killed because they are Hutu and look Tutsi, and even some Tutsis who look like Hutus."

"In Congo we are all Congolese," I said. "It doesn't matter what you look like or where you are from."

After school I would play soccer with my friends in the square near our house. But one day Papa gently warned me not to. "I saw you playing soccer on the street with the boys," he said. "Be careful. As a Muslim girl and the daughter of a prominent member of the community, you shouldn't be seen playing soccer with boys. If an *imam* sees you, he would complain to me about giving my daughter too much freedom."

"I'll be careful, Papa."

But being rebellious by nature, I didn't stop playing soccer with the boys.

Adventure on the Lake

I remember one day before the wars started, when my best friends, Amani and Kanna, and I were swimming in Lake Tanganyika. The boys were very different from each other, but I liked them both. Amani was very protective of me. Kanna was quiet, but he liked to laugh and loved to impress me.

We were having so much fun I didn't even noticed the time. The sun was going down. We were cold and began to shiver.

"We need to get back home," Kanna said. "I can't feel my legs."

I looked around and realized we were in deep water in the middle of nowhere. We began to panic.

I noticed Amani had been quiet. "Amani, please stay alert," I said. "Are you okay?"

"Mama!" he screamed. "I can't move my feet. I'm trapped. The fishermen's net has caught me."

I swam to the bottom and loosened the net that had tangled up around Amani's feet. As I surfaced, a hippopotamus swam toward me.

"Hippopotamus!" I screamed.

We all started swimming in different directions. I swam farther into the lake toward Burundi, Kanna swam in the middle going south, and Amani swam toward the Congolese shore. The hippopotamus swam after me.

"Faster, faster, swim faster, Leolina!" Amani shouted. Then he made loud noises, trying to confuse the hippo.

"Faster, faster!" Kanna was screaming too.

As I thrashed around, I heard the throb of an engine. It was Papa with Kanna's father coming to our rescue. They'd been out on the boat searching for us. Luckily, the hippopotamus had swum away, scared off.

"There's Leolina!" Papa shouted, as they picked up Kanna and then Amani.

Finally they reached me and hoisted me into the boat.

Friday Mornings
at Maison Rouge

Every Friday morning in those days before the wars, we opened up our back garden washroom and shower for our neighbours to use. So I would wake up every Friday to their shouts and curses and the clanging of pots.

Oh no! The washroom wars!

My neighbours screamed and threw their water pots at each other: "Boom!" "Yoweeeh!" "Ohoo, oh!" "Weeeeh!"

I would rush to the back of the garden where the washroom and showers were located to try to sort things out. But to no avail.

One Friday morning, I made up my mind to put a stop to the nonsense once and for all.

"Leolina, stop right there," Maman called to me, as I rushed out in my nightdress.

But she was too late. I was already where the crowd was pushing and pulling and throwing water at each other. Everyone was competing to be first to use our washroom.

"I was here first!" screamed a man draped with a yellow towel, blocking the shower room door.

"I was here before you!" shouted another man in a long, dark red robe.

They pushed and pulled at each other, while blocking doors.

"Stop fighting, stop it please," I called out, but no one paid attention to me.

"Please do something, Leolina," Bibi added.

I picked up an empty five-litre metal oil container, grabbed a stick and struck it hard against the container. Bang! Bang!

Everyone covered their ears and stopped.

"You are fighting with each other like goats!"

"Not everyone has his or her own bathroom like you do!" someone shouted out.

"One thing is for sure. You all need to stop fighting over the toilet and shower every Friday morning," I said, standing my ground.

"Are you saying that we fight *every* Friday?" the man with the yellow towel asked.

"That's right," I said. "And it's got to stop!"

"She's got a point," my schoolmate, Amani, said, stepping out from the crowd. "We are not goats. We need to line up calmly."

"I agree with both the young man and Leolina," the angry fellow in the red robe said, stepping aside for the man in the yellow towel to go in front of him. "You go first."

Just then Papa came out. "Who among you wants to carry water from the river?"

The river was 12 kilometres away.

No one said anything. They were ashamed now about their behaviour.

"Hey, Leolina, you are going to be late for school," my mom called.

I hurried inside and got ready.

War in Burundi

It was late October 1993, just after the rains started. Uvira is on Congo's border with Burundi, and Burundi was at war.

Smoke filled the air—smoke from across the border on the other side of the lake, in our sister city, Bujumbura.

Tina, Mata, Sofia and I climbed the hill above our school to see what was happening over there. All I could see were flames. It sickened me, the thought of burning cities and towns filled with innocent children, elders, men and women.

"I want to go home." I was inconsolable. I couldn't hold back my sense of alarm and terror any longer. I walked away from my friends, down the hill back to school, and they followed.

I just wanted to put my arms around my father.

Back in the classroom, we were consumed with the thought of the bombs and smoke. I hated that the lake was between our city and Bujumbura. I hated that we couldn't help.

"Leolina, why are you looking outside?" our teacher asked. "You are distracting the class again." But the sound of the explosions got louder and louder, and soon all the students ran outside.

"Oh my God!" Sanam yelled. She closed her eyes and prayed.

I ran to the headmaster's office.

I met him at the door, as he was leaving. "Sir, please let us go home."

"Yes. I think that would be best."

I didn't wait for permission from him, but quickly ran to the big bell in the schoolyard. I picked up the metal bar and hit the bell very hard, again and again. All the students ran outside with their school bags.

Classes were over for the day.

Refugees began streaming into our town from Burundi. They were exhausted, hungry and becoming ill. Soon they began to descend on Maison Rouge. The tap water was now reserved for drinking and for strict household necessities. There were so many people now living at our home, all the bathing and washing of dishes and clothes had to be done at the lake.

Every day my friends and I tended to the refugees. We picked all our oranges, lemons and avocados. We made drinks and took them down to Mulongwe, where we knew many of the refugees were gathered. We gave drinks and *beignets* to those tired and hungry people.

I remember one particular day when I approached a woman lying on the ground.

"Aunty, let me help you," I said.

"My back and legs hurt from walking two days with no stop. My stomach is empty. And my heart hurts. They killed my husband, and my daughter is missing."

"Here, please drink this." I gave her some orange juice.

"You know, you look the same age as my daughter."

"Let me give you something to eat," I said, handing her a samosa.

She put the entire samosa in her mouth. I prayed she wouldn't choke. She coughed a little. "Thank you."

We brought her back to Maison Rouge, and after a few days she managed to gain some strength.

One morning she stopped me before I left for school. "Please find my daughter. I lost her at the border." She handed me a picture of her daughter. "This is her."

Her eyes filled with tears.

"After school I will meet with my friends. We will try our best to find her."

"Oh, thank you. Thank you," she said. "May God help you."

We'll need all the help we can get, I thought.

The Border Rescue

Amani, Tina, Zaina, Mata, Indu and Sanam met up with me after school.

"Who would like to go on a mission?" I asked.

"What kind of a mission?" Amani asked.

"A border rescue mission," I explained.

"I'm out," Sanam said.

"That's good. I would be happier to go by myself than to end up having to rescue you too."

"I'll come," Amani said.

"I'll come too," Tina said.

"So will I," Zaina piped in.

"Me too," Indu said.

"I need to go home," Mata said. "My maman will be looking for me."

We walked and walked.

"I can't go any further," Tina said.

Just then a car pulled up. It was Miayo, Zaina's cousin. "What can I do for the young ladies?" he asked. "Zaina, where are you going at this hour?"

"We need your help, please," Zaina said.

"We're helping a refugee woman staying with us find her daughter," I said. "She is stuck at the border."

"What are you waiting for? Get in before I change my mind."

When we reached the border, it was crowded with men, women and children who had fled Burundi. Many were unable to walk, while others just sat waiting for loved ones they had left behind. We were more afraid of the Congolese military than the fighters on the Burundi side. We were not allowed to cross.

"If you try to cross," a soldier said, "I will arrest you."

"You would lock us up?" I asked.

"You heard me."

I tried to explain about the refugee woman's daughter, but he wouldn't listen.

"We can't go on from here," Miayo said. "I'm going back home."

And he drove away, leaving us in the dark.

Another border army guard escorted us to an office.

"You, what are you doing here?" a border inspector asked. "Mr Omar's daughter. I can't believe my eyes."

"Sir, we are only trying to help find a lost girl," I said.

"Does your father know you are here?" the inspector asked.

"Yes . . . " Zaina said.

"No, sir," I interjected.

"I will call him and tell him that you and your friends are here."

"Sorry, sir, you can't do that," I said.

"And why is that?"

"Because we promised a woman to find her lost daughter," I said, "and we need your help."

"Come, I will take you," the inspector said. "Follow me."

We all squeezed into his jeep, and he took off. But then he did a U-turn and drove away from the border.

"Sir, where are you taking us?" I asked him.

"Home."

"But, sir . . ."

He took us back to Maison Rouge.

"Here is your *amana*," he said to Papa, who came out to greet him.

I ran inside Maison Rouge.

A moment later, I came back with a glass of orange juice and stood near the inspector on our veranda.

"Mr Omar . . ." the inspector began.

"Here, have some cold juice, sir," I interrupted.

He took the glass of juice and began to drink.

Meanwhile, I ran back into the dining room. On the table, there was a big plate of fruit. I quickly grabbed some avocados, bananas and mangos and ran back outside to the veranda.

"Mr Omar . . ." he was starting to explain.

But I interrupted him again. "Here are some fruits, sir, for you and your family."

"Oh! Thank you, Leolina," the inspector said

as I gave him the fruit.

"You are welcome, sir," I said. "Bye now, sir. You know, those are not just avocados, sir, they're very special avocados."

"Oh, how is that?"

"My grandma sent the fruit seeds to me, and I planted them myself. They are the best avocados from my mother's village. So now you know. Thank you, and goodbye, sir."

"Mr Omar, I think your daughter wants me to go," the inspector said.

"Well, go enjoy the fruit with your family," my father said.

The inspector got up to leave. "Good night," he said, winking.

Papa suspected something was not right and that I was hiding something. "Leolina, you know you can tell me anything that bothers you."

"I know, Papa. Thank you." I was watching to make sure the inspector left.

The War in Rwanda and Burundi

One morning about six months later—in April, after the rains had stopped—Papa heard on the BBC that the new president of Burundi and the president of Rwanda had been killed after their plane was shot down over Kigali.

I went to school, and the headmaster, Father Dunia, came into our classroom. We all stood up. He gestured for us to take our seats and began talking to us in a soft voice. "I'm afraid that a terrible war has started in Burundi and Rwanda. It could soon spill over to us here in Uvira."

"It's because the Tutsis are fighting with Hutus," our teacher added.

Father Dunia nodded. "Now both peoples have become refugees in the Congo."

Refugees indeed began to stream into Uvira. As Father Dunia had predicted, things got much worse. Commandos arrived and began patrolling the city.

Over the next two years, refugees continued to pour in from Burundi and Rwanda. Some would be carrying mattresses and bags of their worldly possessions on their heads. Others carried children in slings on their backs. Some were elderly, and so tired they just sat any place they could find to rest.

Yayabo

It was October and the rainy season had just begun. I was thirteen years old. The wars in our region had been raging for three years, first in Burundi, then the terrible genocide in Rwanda and then a civil war in Congo, which had now reached all the way to Uvira.

Papa was raking under the fruit trees in the garden.

"Papa," I said, "I met a lady and her daughter who need our help. They have lost everything in the fighting."

"Bring them here, into the garden."

I took a silver container and poured water on my father's hands before he met our new guests.

"This is Papa," I said to the woman.

"I am Omar. What is your name, ma'am?"

"Yayabo," she answered.

"Welcome, Yayabo. You and your daughter can stay as long as you need to."

"Thank you, sir," the woman said, smiling.

Papa could banish sadness from people's faces and give them hope. I brought them to one of the guest rooms. It had its own washroom. I gave them clean clothes.

"From today, this is your home."

"Salaam, I am Leonie Cibibi." Maman greeted Yayabo and her daughter. "Please have a seat. Here is your breakfast."

When my Maman brought food to her, Yayabo fell on my mother's feet and cried.

Maman was embarrassed, so she knelt down and helped her stand up. "Please, I think you would have helped us and done the same if we were in a situation like yours. Let me know if you need anything. Feel at home.

"Leolina, it's time to go to school," she added.

Some time later, as I stepped out of our red gate, my cousin Brown came up to me. "Leolina, I need to talk to you. I have a bad feeling about that woman, Yayabo. I don't think she is who she says she is."

I ignored him, but he walked with me to school.

"Leolina, please hear me out. Someone told me she is deceitful. Be careful."

Brown was right. Our guest, Yayabo, turned out not to be the kind woman we thought she was.

She began by harassing our dog and cat. Then she started yelling at Bibi, the elderly woman who Maman was taking care of in our home. Everyone at Maison Rouge grew frightened of her.

Worse still, Yayabo brought in rebel soldiers to stay overnight with her.

She had shown us her true colours. Eventually she and her daughter were asked to leave our compound. They moved into the house of a neighbour.

Later she would turn out to be the one who betrayed my father to the rebel soldiers who took him away and out of my life forever.

The First Congo War

One day about two years later, Zaina and Amani came home with me from school.

When we arrived at Maison Rouge, it was already dark. There were people crowded outside the main gate and inside the compound in the garden. All around me was chaos. The air was filled with the cries and screams of children, women and men. Some had been shot. Some had burns.

"Leolina!" It was Papa calling. My head was spinning and I was going in circles, overwhelmed and in tears as I stumbled over the wounded.

"I can't see, Papa," I said, falling into his arms. He held me and carried me to my tree—the one with both lemons and oranges.

Papa knew that if I sat under that tree, its sweet aroma would calm me down.

"Leolina, get hold of yourself! This isn't the time to cry. Gather your courage."

I couldn't stop, so Papa said, "It's okay to cry, but don't lose heart, because these people need you. Pull yourself together. Let's go and comfort them. You be the doctor."

Papa often used to call me "doctor" because I was good at caring for sick family, friends and neighbours. "Yes," I said. "I'll be the doctor." I was relieved to be given a task to do.

"Let's go, my brave princess." My father took my hand and led me through our garden to the house. "Take a deep breath, in and out."

I picked my way through the tangled bodies. "I'm so sorry," I said, as I stepped over sleeping people.

We gave everyone cold orange juice and lemonade, beignets, samosas and bajias that Maman prepared. Maman also roasted a few chickens and ducks. Everyone ate. We bandaged wounds and put salve on the children's burns. There was nothing else we could do.

After tending to people for hours, I was falling asleep on my feet, so my mother led me to my room. But there were women and children in there, and nowhere to place even a foot. A bunch of girls were bundled on my bed, fast asleep.

I stumbled back outside. Our garden was not a garden anymore but an outdoor kitchen. Maman cooked food there in the huge pots that we normally used only for celebrations. No stove in the house could hold pots that were as big as those.

"I'll be back soon," my father called. "I need to buy more food and firewood."

I followed him out to the driveway. He jumped into our minibus and pulled out. As I watched him drive away, some of my classmates came up.

"Eh! Leolina," Amani said, signalling for me to come and meet him. He was with Mata and Indira in front of our gate.

"Oh Lord, God of mercy. Look at all these people!" exclaimed Tina.

"Yeah, eh!" Indira exclaimed. "My grandpa told me it was like this in India before they escaped to the Congo after independence."

"It's terrible," I said. "So much suffering."

"All the neighbours are talking about how your father and mother welcomed so many refugees to your home," Mata said.

"Maison Rouge is a refugee camp now," Amani said. "It's not an elegant mansion anymore."

We are Refugees

As conditions worsened, Papa decided that we needed to leave Maison Rouge. His friend in Kigoma, Tanzania—on the other side of Lake Tanganyika—was willing to put our family up until things settled down.

We stayed a while, but the fighting in the Congo went on and on, so we decided to try to go to South Africa via Zambia. Unfortunately, the Zambian immigration authorities handed us over to the UN, and we became resident in a UNHCR refugee camp.

The fighting had died down temporarily and so in December, we left Zambia and went to Lubumbashi in the Congo. From there we travelled back to Uvira by buses and trains. Maman was pregnant with my baby brother, Moise. New Year's Day 1997 was spent en route. One month or so later, we arrived back in Maison Rouge. Sarafina was there to greet us.

Child Soldiers

Amani had been missing for several days. My friends and I went to look for him at his grandpa's house, but the door was locked. Amani had been living there for the past while, as his mother had left the city and returned to her village.

We asked around, but our neighbours wouldn't tell us anything. There was nowhere else we could look for him, so we started back.

"Wait a second, are you guys seeing what I am seeing?" Saja asked.

I looked and there was a group of boys our age in military uniform, walking in rank in front of us. At the head were some men, carrying guns and machetes.

I couldn't believe my eyes.

I walked up to the marching boys. One of them was shouting, "One hundred metres!"

"Amani?" I said, stopping in the middle of the road.

It was Amani, but he looked like a zombie.

"One hundred metres!" he yelled again, and shot his gun in the air. The soldiers stopped and pointed their guns at me. I froze. Mata pulled me away.

I was incredulous—devastated to see my friend had turned into a child soldier.

"You, little girl. You want to hug the ground?" a soldier shouted at me.

"What did you do to my Amani?" I asked him.

"Amani isn't your friend anymore. We are his family now."

As they marched away, I called after them, "Amani, Amani, what happened to you? What's wrong with you, Amani?"

Amani turned back and looked at me. His zombie eyes sparked with recognition for a brief moment.

"Let's go, Leolina." Sanam and Mata grabbed my hand and led me off down the road.

I realized then that Amani had shot in the air to save me. Otherwise one of the other solidiers might have shot me.

Still, I had lost my friend. I couldn't stop thinking about Amani at school and Amani at the river and Amani at the lake and at Maison Rouge—all our laughter, all the good times.

I trudged back to Maison Rouge, heartbroken.

The Major

When I reached Maison Rouge, I took *hudhu*, or ablutions, washing my hands, face and feet before I prayed.

I lifted my hands to God and asked for another chance to meet my friend Amani. And I prayed for all people suffering from the war.

But I was not at peace. I went outside.

Bibi was standing by the gate. "Leolina, where are you going?"

"I'm going to Zabibu's house." Zabibu was one of my new girlfriends who had escaped the war in Burundi.

"Change out of those jeans," Bibi said.

"What do you mean?" I asked her.

"Now that the rebel leader Kabila has taken over, his soldiers are beating girls for wearing jeans."

"Now the soldiers decide what girls can and cannot wear?" I said.

I kept going.

"Don't say I didn't warn you," Bibi shouted after me.

Two soldiers stopped me at a checkpoint just down the road.

"Go change your clothes," one soldier said.

"Are you talking to me?" I asked him.

"Yeah, go and change those pants," he said.

"Why?"

"It is a new law," the second soldier explained. "Girls and women aren't allowed to wear pants."

"So that they won't rule the world?" I muttered.

"What did you say?" the first soldier demanded.

"Mobutu doesn't care if girls or women wear pants," I said. "I forgot he isn't the president any more."

"You think you're so smart."

They took me into their military jeep and drove me to their headquarters.

An officer was sitting outside. "Why are you arresting this young girl?" he asked.

"She refused to go home and change into a dress, Major," one of the soldiers answered.

"Come, have a seat." The Major gestured for me to sit down. "The soldiers are just following orders. Oh, but aren't you Leolina? Your Papa is a noble and good man. He helped my family, and paid for my sister's education. Today she is a doctor and helps thousands of women."

"I will be just like your sister. Papa wants me to be a doctor. He says I am good at helping people get well."

"I can believe that."

"One favor, sir."

"Yes, mademoiselle."

"Please release the other girls and women too," I said to him. "That rule about girls wearing pants has never been enforced before."

"Well, I'll think about it."

"Thanks, sir," I said and I smiled.

The Major drove me home, and I shook hands with him. He was a good man. And he never did speak to Papa.

As I entered my bedroom, I noticed a big change. The room was empty. I went back outside into our compound. The crowds that had been staying at Maison Rouge had fled. Only a few people were left, including Sarafina, Bibi, Fundi and the others living in our outbuildings, plus a few refugees.

"They are gone," Bibi said.

"Where? When?"

"They all asked me to thank you on their behalf," Maman said.

"But, they were here when I left for school."

Amani

The next afternoon, I saw a skinny boy sitting on a bench outside our school. I looked closely.

"Amani!" I couldn't believe my eyes. "Amani, is that you?"

It was indeed my friend, Amani, and he and I ran up to each other and hugged tightly.

"Are you back, Amani?"

"Not for too long." His voice was sad. "I am sorry for shooting the bullets at you," he said and started crying.

"Hey, it's okay," I said. "You shot in the air and you saved my life. Those soldiers put a curse on you."

Amani held my hand, and we ran.

"Thank Allah, I have my friend back," I said.

We ran up to a big white mansion.

"Come," Amani gave me a hand and helped me up the stairs.

"What is this place?" I asked.

"It was a rich person's home. But they fled. Now we are taking it over."

At the door, Amani pulled up his sleeve and showed a mark on his right hand to the soldier who was at the door. The soldier let us inside.

"What's that mark on your hand?"

"It is nothing." He didn't want to explain it to me.

"It looks like a tattoo."

"It's your name, Leolina," he said.

"My name is on your hand? But why?"

Amani led us into a dark room where a movie was in progress. We watched it until the end.

"Thanks, Amani, that was nice," I said.

"Come," Amani said. "I'll bring you home."

"Are you coming back?" I asked him.

Suddenly, a pair of combat jets started dropping bombs, and a bomb hit not far from where Amani and I were standing.

"*Mayi, mayi!* Water, water!" he shouted, pushing me down for cover.

It felt like time had stopped. I was terrified.

Then people started moving again.

"Why is Mobutu bombing us, his own people?" I wanted to know.

"That was just a warning to show off his power," Amani said. "That's why I was saying *mayi, mayi*. So that when the bomb exploded, the shrapnel wouldn't hit us."

I shook my head. I didn't get it.

"The elders put spells on us to protect us warriors," he continued, "so machetes, bombs and bullets can't harm us. They just fall like water off our skin."

"Please come back. I promise I won't bother you anymore." I tried to convince him.

"No. Never."

"Why not?"

"It's not because of you."

"Why then?" I pulled his ear.

"Ouch, that hurt," he said.

He turned back toward the white mansion, and I grabbed his shoulder.

"Go back to your friends," Amani ordered,

shrugging me off. "I don't know if we will have another chance to see each other in this lifetime again." Tears streaked down Amani's face, and I cried too.

Then suddenly he pulled me close and cried. "Take care, Leolina. I love you!"

Then he ran away.

"Amani, Amani," I called to him. But he had already disappeared.

The Last Good Time

One Saturday afternoon, after the rainy season had started, Papa drove me to the Yogurt Palace, where they served special French patisserie and yogurts. Papa and I were welcomed, and I ate almost a litre of yogurt by myself. We had such a good time. I told some jokes and Papa laughed and laughed.

That would be the last good time I would have with my papa.

On the way back, traffic was held up by a convoy of UN Food Program trucks rolling into Uvira. Some trucks were filled with munitions, some with uniformed boys and girls—armed tyrant-soldiers. Others were loaded with dead bodies.

The sun was no longer shining warm and clear. The air felt cold and smelled of blood.

The wars had begun in earnest. In the streets, no busy merchants prepared to sell their wares. Soon the churches closed, and the morning church bells stopped ringing. Only one mosque remained open.

The sun was blood red at its rising and setting.

That Darkest Night

Our hopes for a return to the normal life we knew were shattered.

Late one night, just after the bombing had started, we were awoken by the sound of heavy banging. "Mr Omar, open up."

I ran to the corridor leading up to the front door and watched as Papa opened it to a group of rebel soldiers. They had their guns trained on him.

Sarafina, our housekeeper, came up to me, and we stood with Maman. My brother Raja and sisters Fifi, Mimi and Massy had woken up and snuck in behind me. Our baby brother, Moise, slept through it all.

"Are you Sir Omar?" the leader of the commandos asked.

"Yes, I am," said Papa. "Why this late visit? Come back in the morning."

"You must come now, sir," he said, grabbing Papa by the arm.

Papa called out to us, "I won't be long."

"Take anything you want from the house," Maman cried to the soldiers. She rushed to Papa. "But please let my husband go."

Papa pulled loose from the soldier's grip and took Maman in his arms.

"I'll come with you," she said.

Papa kissed her on her forehead and whispered something in her ear.

One of the commandos pulled him back out into the street.

"Papa!" I called out.

"Leolina, don't worry! I'll be back by sunrise."

Maman ran after them calling back to me, "Leolina, take care of your sisters and brothers until I return."

I slipped onto the floor crying. My young sisters and brother hugged me.

"Don't cry," Sarafina said. "I will take care of you all until your parents come back."

I got up and took hold of the girls' hands, and we turned down the corridor to my room.

"Don't worry, Leolina," my sister Fifi said, trying to cheer me up.

The commandos had taken our papa away.

I lay down on my bed and cried myself to asleep.

That night, I dreamt Papa was living in a big stone cave.

"Papa, Maison Rouge is your house."

In my dream, I crossed over to him. He stood in front of the cave, stopping me from entering. He gathered me in his arms and said, "Your mother is in prison, Leolina. Rescue her." Then Papa told me the name of the prison, before disappearing into the stone cave.

I woke up shouting, "Papa!"

Papa had a heart of gold; he lived only for other people. Every day I am grateful that he was able to share his wisdom with me.

"Leolina, wake up!" Bibi was shaking me, and I heard the *hadhan* calling *fajir*, the early morning prayer. It felt like time had stopped and had turned my world upside down. But I came to my senses. I quickly dressed and rushed to Papa and Maman's bedroom.

Sarafina was making the bed.

"Your maman never came back," she said, crying. "I'm frightened."

"They took her to prison," I said to her.

"How do you know?" she asked.

"Papa told me in my dream."

I raced out of Maison Rouge. I ran and ran until I reached the prison where Papa had told me in the dream that Maman was being held. I pushed open the big wooden door.

A jail guard stood there smoking. "My mother is locked up here," I said, breathless. "I am Sir Omar's daughter."

On overhearing this, the Major approached, the same one who had driven me home before.

"Leolina, why are you here?" he asked.

"Maman is being held prisoner here."

The Major brought me to his office. "Your parents are the most respected people in Uvira. They are pillars of our community. I didn't know your maman was here. The commandos must have taken her." He called the guard and ordered him to bring Maman to him.

Tears ran down my face. I ran to her. She had bruises and cuts on her legs, hands and face. My heart felt like it was being pulled out of my chest.

Papa's last words rang in my ears. "Leolina, take care of your mother and your sisters and brothers until I return."

I supported Maman as she limped outside. "Have you taken good care of your brothers and sisters?"

"Yes, Maman."

"Have you heard anything about Papa?"

I stifled a cry. "No, nothing."

"You must be strong, Leolina. These are dangerous times."

I stared at her cuts and bruises and

understood. I swallowed my tears, pushed back my shoulders and straightened my spine. We staggered back to Maison Rouge.

The next day, we heard from neighbours that militias were taking boys, some of them very young, away from their families.

After morning prayers Maman took me aside. "I'm taking Massy and Moise to look for your father. Dress up Raja to look like a girl. I don't want to risk taking him outside." Then she turned to Sarafina. "Please look after the girls and little Raja, Sarafina. You are like a sister to me."

"I will, madame," Sarafina said, holding back her tears.

Maman turned to me again. "Leolina, take care of your sisters and your little brother. We will come back after I find your papa."

Then Maman strapped Moise to her back and left, holding Massy's little hand. We quickly dressed Raja in Mimi's clothes.

The very next morning, my neighbours burst through the front door, crying. "They killed him!" they howled. "Your Papa is no more."

I screamed. In my heart, I felt the most pain I had ever felt and will ever feel. Sarafina held me tight. Everyone was wailing.

"Your Papa," Sarafina said, "was the most beautiful soul I ever met."

The Fall of Maison Rouge

Soldiers had been going from house to house, taking all the boys and men away—even the very young and very old—and putting them into trucks. The new soldiers were tall, so they must have been Tutsi. We didn't know if they were from Rwanda or Burundi.

Later that day before the sun went down, we heard gunshots. Soldiers stormed into our house to search. They looked under the beds and in the closets, shouting. But only me, Sarafina, Mimi, Fifi, and Raja—dressed like a girl—were there.

We later heard that the rebel militias had taken all the boys and men they had rounded up to the stadium and had shot them.

Gunshots rang out throughout the city. Everyone ran inside and hid wherever they could. War had broken out between the Kabila government soldiers and the rebel militias from Rwanda and Uganda.

Mimi, Fifi and my little brother Raja were huddled together with me in my bedroom. Sarafina was in Maman and Papa's room.

Loud voices and shouts rang from the street outside.

I opened the window a crack.

"Who are they?" Fifi whispered.

"They're soldiers," I said, slowly closing it. "They have bullets and grenades slung across their jackets. Some of them are carrying rockets."

"How many soldiers are there?" Fifi asked.

"Hundreds. And more soldiers are coming in military pickups and jeeps."

My heart raced. Then a chill shook me. I felt so cold—like being frozen alive.

Something was wrong, very wrong. I could sense something bad was happening.

"Get out!" I shouted, holding Raja, who was dressed in Mimi's nightgown. Quickly, I jumped up and pushed my sisters out the bedroom door, following them into the corridor.

Just in time.

Seconds later, a rocket smashed into the bedroom. The earth shook and Maison Rouge burst into flames. We huddled, dazed and terrified.

It seemed like time had stopped. I couldn't tell if I was dead or alive.

Then everything went silent—absolutely silent. There was not even a dog barking, just the crackle of fire.

My sisters were lying face down on the ground, covered with black dust from head to toe.

"Fifi! Mimi!" I whispered. "Are you alive?" Raja was crying in my arms.

"Fifi, wake up!" I shook her and she started to move. I shook Mimi, and she stirred too. My sisters were alive.

"Thanks be to Allah."

I picked my way through the rubble into what was left of Maman and Papa's room. Sarafina was buried under concrete. She didn't move.

I held Raja tightly and ran with my sisters through the smoke out of what was left of the house. Our beloved Maison Rouge was in flames, and dear Sarafina was dead. Papa was in the other world. We were homeless and we had no news of Maman, Massy and Moise.

We had lost everything.

We walked to the lakeshore without looking back. "Where are Maman, Massy and Moise? Are they going to come soon?" Fifi asked me.

"Don't worry." I answered. "We will find them."

"Promise," Mimi said.

"Yes, promise," I said to her.

"Where will we go?" Mimi asked.

"To Maman's cousin's house along the lake. Maman might be there."

I held my young sisters' hands, and we started

walking south as fast as we could—along the lake, away from Uvira toward the port in Kabindula.

"Allah, protect and guide us," I prayed.

We kept walking until nighttime, finally reaching Kabindula where Maman's cousin lived. There were soldiers everywhere, walking back and forth, looking like zombies. Their faces were painted in red and black. They were speaking in Kinyarwanda and Kirundi, languages that I didn't understand.

When we reached the house, Maman's cousin was standing in front.

"Leolina, Mimi, Fifi," she said, hugging us. "And who's this little girl," she said, pointing at Raja.

"It's Raja," I said. "We dressed him like a girl. They took all the boys and men away."

"Hush!" she said, putting her finger to her lips. "Come inside.

"And your Papa and Maman?" she said, as

we sat down on the wooden chairs in the sparse kitchen.

"Maman doesn't know that Papa is dead. And she doesn't know that Maison Rouge is no more."

"It's a terrible time."

"Maman went with Moise and Massy to find Papa."

"God willing, they're safe."

The Longest One-Way Road

It was noon and very hot. There were many wounded. We were thousands and thousands, walking in file, south along the lake. We couldn't pass or step out of line. The mass of people pushed us forward.

I heard a man calling. "Leolina, Fifi, Mimi, Raja!" It was my Uncle Mura, Maman's brother. He was holding the hand of my sister Massy.

Mimi hugged him. "Uncle!" I hugged Massy. My Uncle Mura walked with us, holding Fifi and Mimi's hands.

"Where is Maman, Uncle?" I asked him.

"She's way back there somewhere."

As I scanned the throng, hoping to catch a glimpse of her, someone shouted: "Look, a submarine!"

I turned toward the lake as bullets sprayed the crowd and everyone scrambled for cover.

A bullet grazed my knee.

"Get down, Raja," I screamed, covering him as well as I could with my body.

I ripped a piece of fabric from my headscarf and tied it around the wound to stop it from bleeding.

I called to my sisters, "Fifi, Mimi, stay here!" But my uncle had them.

"Don't worry!" he shouted. "I'll take care of them." Then he was lost in the panicking crowd.

People were screaming out in pain and fear. Children got separated from their parents. Blood and fire, pain and death were everywhere.

Suddenly everything went quiet. Massy sobbed, holding me tight. Raja clung to me.

Just then a fighter plane swooped down out of a bank of clouds and began to fire on the panicking crowd. We were trapped—thousands of us stuck between the mountain and the lake on a dirt track not wide enough for a jeep to pass.

Some people jumped into the lake.

"We can't stay here." I pat down my brother and sister from head to toes to see if they were okay.

We stepped over an elderly woman, who had fallen. She was clutching a silver pot. I reached down to help her up.

"Bibi?" I was shocked to see her, relieved that she had not died from the bombardment of Maison Rouge.

She placed the pot on her head.

"Why are you carrying that pot?" I asked her. "Just throw it away."

She joined us as we walked, the pot balanced on her head.

We kept walking until we reached the end of the road. Near the lake, there were lots of mango trees. I helped Bibi sit under a big one.

"An old woman like me doesn't need to live," Bibi said.

"Who says?" I said to her.

"My grandson. I took care of him since he

was a baby when his mother died in the hospital. Now he considers me to be a burden and calls me a worthless old woman."

"Please Bibi, don't cry. Come, let's go. You are our Bibi and my family and I will never let you go again. Papa and Maman love you and we all do."

And then I remembered Papa. And I cried my heart out.

"Papa is dead," I said. "Killed by the rebel soldiers."

"And Maman?"

"She is back there," I said, pointing. "Uncle Mura has Fifi and Mimi. He will find Maman."

"These are terrible times, my child. Leave me here. I can't walk anymore. My feet are swollen."

"Try to walk slowly," I insisted.

"No, you just go along," Bibi said. "I'll wait here until your maman and your uncle reach me, and I'll go with them. You go, Leolina, go with your brother and sister."

"But Bibi . . ."

"Please take this," Bibi said, handing me the

silver pot and a bottle of water. "I have another one. There are peas in the pot. Now go."

I carried the pot of peas on my head and tied Massy to my back. We reached a small track between the lake and the mountain. It was very hard to walk without slipping into the lake, which was deep and dangerous. And there was no way to climb the mountain.

I tried to force Massy and Raja to eat the peas, but they refused. I climbed a mango tree and picked a mango, even though it was not quite ripe. Raja and Massy ate it. I saw a girl crying and asking people if they had seen her young brother.

I recognized her as one of our neighbours. "Nelly?" I called out to her.

"Did you see my young brother, Leolina?"

"No," I said. "But don't lose hope. I am sure he is fine and you will find him."

"How do you know?"

"I have faith in God," I said.

"I wish I was like you, Leolina, but I'm not," Nelly said.

"*Dada?*" my younger brother called. "Never leave me, big sister."

"I won't, Raja," I promised him.

"I know, Dada," Raja hugged me. Massy hugged me too.

I was sitting with my young brother and sister under the mango tree, and out of nowhere a tall white man stepped up to us, dropping to the ground. It was very hot in the midday sun.

"*Ici et en qu'en France c'est combien de kilometres?*" the Frenchman asked. "How many kilometres from here to Paris?"

"I don't know," I replied in French.

But the Frenchman kept repeating the same question. He held a water bottle in his hand, and there were a few drops left. I held his head, opened his mouth and gave him the little water he had left. It was almost as hot as tea. I ran to the lake, got some water and poured it on his head. Then he sat up.

"What's your name?" the Frenchman asked me.

"Leolina."

"You are like an angel," he said.

"No, I'm not," I answered.

A stream of refugees was passing by us. Among them I recognized my friend, Safi. She came up to us. "Leolina, I saw your maman back there, not far away."

"You are a good friend, Safi." I was so thankful to hear news about Maman.

"And Moise, Fifi and Mimi and your uncle and your maman's cousin are with her," she added.

I hugged and thanked her.

"Thanks, Safi. May Allah be with you."

"Allah be with you and your family, Leolina."

"You are the first person who has helped me," the Frenchman said to me.

"Can you try to walk?" I asked him. "You should keep walking, sir, until you find a boat to go to Tanzania. From there you can find a way to get to Paris."

"Okay, I'll walk with you," the Frenchman said. We headed off.

Soon the moon came out. We went down to the lake, and I poured water on our heads. I splashed a little water at the French man.

"Ah, ahaa!" he yelled. My young brother splashed a little water at him again, and then he stepped into the lake too, with a smile on his face. We were all smiling as we stepped back out of the lake.

I opened the pot of green peas, but they looked and smelled so bad. "I am not hungry," Raja said, as he looked at the peas.

"Me either," Massy said, pinching her nose.

"I'll eat them," the Frenchman said, grabbing the pot and starting to eat. Soon his stomach started to growl.

"They're bad," he said, rushing away from us. "Ah, France, it's all your fault!"

We left the Frenchman there and carried on walking in the moonlight, until we reached an abandoned village. All the houses were on fire and there were no signs of life. I saw a mango tree and picked four green mangos. I gave one to Massy and one to Raja. I saw a pregnant woman who was sitting there with a young child, so I gave one mango to her. The green mangos tasted like lemons.

We fell asleep holding hands.

Our Family is Reunited

"Leolina. Oh my daughter!" Maman said, shaking me awake.

"Ma, Ma!" I cried, hugging her.

"Thank Allah, my children are alive!"

Maman took me and my brother and sister to the rest of our family. She had some cooked sweet potatoes and fish that she had bought from a local villager.

The next morning, I bathed in the lake and it felt so good as I hadn't showered for a long time. I put on new green jeans and a pink, long-sleeved shirt that Maman had brought. Then I took a piece of my Maman's wax cloth and covered myself. I prayed, asking Allah to protect us and all the people who suffered.

The nights and days passed, and my family and I kept walking with no clean water and little food.

Our people spent weeks fleeing from the war,

but the war kept following us. At night we rested as best we could, sleeping in the open by Lake Tanganyika.

One morning on waking, I heard a familiar voice shout my name.

It was the Frenchman we had met before, calling from a crowded boat.

"Leolina, *mon ange!*"

"Who is that, my child?" Maman asked.

"He's a Frenchman we met," I said. "He wants to get to Paris."

"Leolina, mon ange!" the Frenchman shouted again. The boat was so overloaded, it tipped back and forth.

"What's his name?" Maman asked.

"I think his name is *Combien*," Raja said.

We all laughed.

The little boat disappeared into the horizon.

"That boat will sink," Maman said.

"I hope not," I said, as it disappeared from view. "I hope that man reaches Paris."

One night, I lit a little fire. It was chilly, and we had no blankets.

"Wake up, Dada," Massy said, shaking me. But I was so tired, I thought it was a dream.

I opened my eyes, finally.

"Leolina, don't move!" Maman said. She was flicking a big black spider off my belly.

"Thank you, Maman," I said, hugging her.

Then holding a finger to her lips, she slipped a money belt around me, under my shirt. "This is half our money," she whispered. "I went back to Maison Rouge, and I found it where Papa had hidden it. It will save our lives."

"I will keep it safe, Maman. Don't worry."

We kept on heading south, with the thousands of others fleeing the war. Some were children left without parents. Everyone had only one wish—to stay alive and to reach a place of safety.

River of Blood

After passing several checkpoints, my family and I reached the village of Mboko, a place where the hills and the lake were very close together. Exhausted refugees were gathered there after fleeing the fighting between the Kabila army and the Mobutu government soldiers.

"Stay here, Leolina. Watch over your sisters and brother, and I will be back," Maman said to me. She picked up Moise and walked down to the lakeshore.

Hours later Maman came back with a boy I knew from school. His name was Dan, and his father was a fisherman. He knew Papa.

"Dan's father has a boat," Maman said to us. "I paid him to take us across the lake to safety in Tanzania. Hurry."

We followed Dan and Maman down to the beach.

"Mrs Omar, we have to hurry. We must start

boarding," the fisherman said.

As we were gathering, we heard the roar of an approaching jet. It made one pass, circled back and fired into the crowd. Soon it was joined by another, and they started to bomb us. It felt like the mountain was exploding. People jumped into the lake, but they were strafed by the jets. Just as a piece of shrapnel grazed my forehead, Maman threw herself over us, screaming, "On the ground, face down."

As I dropped onto the beach, blood filled my eyes. I felt cold and passed out. When I came to there was an old man looking down at me gesturing wildly. He had come up to us out of nowhere. "Follow me and don't look back," he said. "Hurry!"

My maman picked up Moise and followed the old man. Crouching low to avoid the bombing, my sisters trailed behind; and, though I wasn't able to see clearly, I managed to stumble after them.

Finally, the man pointed to the door of a

tumble-down mud house.

"Go in there and be quiet," he said.

We rushed in. I touched my forehead, and found the bleeding had stopped.

The planes finally flew away, as quickly as they had come. Peeking through the door, I saw burning trees. After some time, Maman went outside and signalled for us to follow. "Come quickly."

We walked until it was dark. I met Safi. She was overcome with grief. Her entire family had been killed on that beach.

We came across Dan, who was carrying his two-year-old baby brother. "My father's boat, the one your family was about to board, has been sunk," Dan said. "My father is dead. I'm going back to Uvira. I can't run anymore."

I never saw him again.

We walked for a week. Our feet were swollen. We were hungry and thirsty and tired. We hurried through a small ghost village where only three people, with serious burns, had survived the bombing and strafing.

Soon we came upon bodies upon bodies strewn across a field. A river of blood flowed into a nearby stream, turning it scarlet.

I felt lost, as if a dark cloud had descended over me.

"Maman, why are all these people sleeping?" my little brother Raja asked.

She didn't answer. "Keep walking, my children. Don't look."

We held hands and tried to avoid stepping on the bodies. I felt a deep pain in my heart. "Oh, God!" I cried.

Vultures circled overhead.

Taken Hostage

In Baraka, Maman went to buy something to eat, while I waited with my young sisters and brother. Soon she came back with fish and roe, and we made fufu with cassava root, steamed inside banana leaves.

After my siblings fell asleep, Maman said, "I found another boat that will take us to Tanzania. The captain is a friend of your Papa."

She asked me for my money belt and took half the money. "I gave Dan's father all the money I had, Leolina."

There were government soldiers everywhere. One of them came up to us. It was the Major who had released Maman from jail. "Hello, Leolina," he greeted me. "Hello Madame."

Mama shook his hand. "Major," she said. "I can never thank you enough for releasing me from prison."

"As you know, I was a good friend of your esteemed husband, Omar, may he rest in peace," he said. "Leolina, you can call me Uncle."

"Thank you, Uncle Major," I said, giving him a hug.

"How much will the trip cost, Maman?"

"All the money I have," Maman said, winking at me.

That day we had our first good solid food and fresh water to drink in weeks. In the evening, our boat left for Tanzania. We prayed that our journey would be safe.

After we pulled out into deep water, the captain announced, "Soon, we will leave Congolese waters."

People were happy, and some women started singing, "Hallelujah!" Others replied, "Amen." They were Christian women from Uvira, and they sang in Swahili.

We were far out in the lake, when suddenly

we heard the rapid fire of machine guns. The captain turned the engine off, and the women stopped singing.

Bullets flew over our heads. More gunfire.

"Get down!" the captain shouted.

Soon rebel troops, dressed in black fatigues, pulled up in their boat pointing machine guns.

"Turn the engine on," one of them ordered.

"I will give you money," the captain said, "but let us go."

"That's exactly what we want," one soldier shouted.

The leader leapt aboard our boat and struck the captain with his gun. Blood poured from the wound. Everyone screamed. Then two more rebels jumped aboard, their guns pointed at us. "Don't move! If you move, you are dead."

The leader started the engine, and drove our boat to their camp on a small cove. Their boat followed.

"All of you, get out!" the leader ordered.

People walked along the boat deck, passing

their children to the men who were helping everyone off the boat. Women jumped into the water and held their babies up in the air while they struggled to shore. When we got to the beach, the rebels shot their guns in the air.

"All of you lie down," the rebel leader said. "Anyone who moves or speaks is dead."

"Keep your heads down!" another one of the zombies shouted, firing in the air.

They began to search the men's pockets, and took the women's earrings, gold chains, bracelets and watches.

"Where is the money?" one of the rebels shouted to the captain, who was still on board his boat.

"Here!" he shouted, holding up a sack.

With my head half-buried in the sand, I was able to glimpse our captain fling his sack of money into the lake.

Then the rebel soldiers on board threw off their fatigues and dove into the lake, swimming toward the floating bag. At the same time the boat engine started up. The rebels strafed the boat from the lakeshore as it raced away. Their leader swam back with the bag, shouting, "That liar! The only thing in the bag is some old clothes. Start the engine and go after him!"

But they never did catch up to his boat. And it's a good thing for us that they didn't.

They turned on us. The zombie leader brutally held an elderly woman by her neck, pointing his pistol at her head. "You are wealthy. Give us your money or we will shoot you."

"Please don't kill me," she cried.

Maman whispered to me to give her the money belt I still had under my shirt. "Shii! Don't say a word."

I managed to slip it to her, without drawing the attention of the zombie soldiers.

"Please, stop torturing us," Maman spoke up. "Take this and let her go." She stood up and threw the money to them.

One of them strode over to my maman and pushed her to the ground. "Who are you?"

The rebel turned back to the elderly woman and shot over her head. We all screamed.

"Keep your faces down in the sand!" the leader shouted, opening my money belt and passing the cash around to some of his men and boys.

"Choose the women and girls for yourselves," he announced.

"Please don't take my wife, she's pregnant," a man pleaded.

"Who cares?" another rebel said, ordering the pregnant woman to stand up.

Her husband stood up too, and said, "I am coming with my wife."

"We don't need men," the rebel said, shooting him dead.

Everyone screamed.

"Shut up or you die!" the leader shouted.

Then they started to pick out women and girls. "You stand up," they ordered. "You come with us. You too."

"Let go of my daughter!" Maman shouted, pushing the young rebel off me. He backed off. The rebels took three girls and two women into the forest, and we heard their screams.

"Please," the elderly woman begged, "you are the same age as my grandson,"

One of the rebels approached her. "Get up," he said. "What do you have under your scarf?"

She took off a gold necklace and handed it to him.

Taking the gold necklace, he screamed, "Give me all your money."

"My child, I have given you everything I have. I have no money left."

The rebel turned to a young woman who was seated next to her. "Who is she?" he asked.

"My daughter," she answered. She was shaking. "Please don't harm her."

"All the men stand to the right. And you women and girls move to the left.

"Get up," one of the rebels ordered, pointing

his gun at me. "You are mine. Come here!"

He pushed the muzzle of his gun against my head.

"I am coming too," Maman cried out.

"Please, Maman," I pleaded, "stay with my sisters and brothers."

Just then Raja turned on his little radio. "This is BBC Radio, Tanzania . . ." the announcer said.

"Who is that talking?" one of the rebels shouted.

"Ah, ah!" little Raja laughed.

The zombie rebel went over to Raja, grabbed the radio, threw it on the ground and shot a hail of bullets into it.

"You, come here," the rebels were still choosing women and girls. "Follow me."

"Keep still," one zombie boy soldier said.

"Stop crying," another one shouted.

"Don't turn around!" still another ordered.

They pushed us—girls and women—ahead of them into the forest, leaving two zombie rebels behind at the shore with the men, boys, young girls and older women.

"If anyone tries to run away," the rebel leader shouted, "shoot them!"

"I am coming too!" Maman insisted. She was holding Moise.

My sisters and Raja were all crying.

"Okay, carry this," a young zombie soldier said, passing her a bag.

"Maman!" Fifi cried out.

"We will be back," Maman assured them. "Inshallah. God willing."

We carried everything on our heads and followed the zombie rebels into the mountains. Soon night fell and a full moon rose in the sky above the trees. There were the cries of monkeys and the loud calls of flycatchers overhead. We came to a river and a fresh strong breeze touched me, somehow restoring my hope.

We walked along the river up to the edge of a waterfall and couldn't go any further. Just as I was beginning to wonder if these rebels knew where they were going, one of the girls screamed. She had tripped and fallen into the river.

Without hesitating, I gripped a root with one hand and pulled her upright with the other. Maman came over and steadied me. The poor girl was shattered, and I tried to comfort her.

"Enough!" the rebel leader growled, as he stepped into the riverbed. "Now, let's cross to the other side."

He was up to his waist in the water, and held his rifle over his head. Slowly, he moved to the middle. Some of the girls were shoulder deep in the water. But the current was too fast. One of the soldiers slipped and was swept over the falls, letting out a long cry. Another stepped to its edge, to see what had happened to his comrade. But he too fell to his death.

"We're going back," the leader shouted. So we turned around, slipping on the muddy riverbank.

Back at the lakeshore, the zombie soldiers who were left behind started shooting into the air.

Dawn was breaking, and they lay down to

sleep. Only two or three of them kept guard.

"I remember you," one of the guards said. "Your father ran theatre groups and built schools. I studied at one of them."

"Why are you here with these people?" Maman asked him.

"I was first recruited by the Mobutu army, then the Kabila militias, finally I ended up with these demons. I had no choice."

Rescue

Just then gunshots rang out, and a patrol boat landed. Dozens of government soldiers disembarked and fanned out, surrounding the zombie rebels.

"Don't be afraid," an officer shouted. "We are here to rescue you."

One of the zombies made a break for the forest. "*Mayi, mayi!* Water, water!" he shouted.

A burst of gunfire, and he fell screaming to the sand.

"Put down your guns," the rebel leader shouted, holding up his hands in surrender. With that, the zombie rebels stopped shooting and everything went quiet.

The officer shouted to his soldiers, "Hold your fire!"

The bullets had skinned the fallen zombie's head, and he was bleeding and screaming in terror.

"That is how you made the girls feel," a women screamed at him. "So, now you feel the pain."

"I am sorry," he pleaded.

"These men and boys will pay for their crimes," the officer said. "Bring them here."

The soldiers stood them on the sand in front of us. Their hands were clasped to their heads and their ankles were tied with ropes. Their eyes were lowered, so as not to look at the face of any of the women or girls.

"Papa said to forgive," I said to the one who had held a gun to my head. "So I do forgive you."

"He was going to sacrifice you, Leolina." the elderly woman said. "How can you forgive him?"

Just then the officer came up to me.

"Uncle Major, it's you," I said. It was the same officer who had released my Maman from prison, and who met us just before we left on the fisherman's boat.

"Yes, Leolina, it is." His face took on a worried look. "Did he touch you?"

"No, he didn't. He didn't rape me, but he raped

other girls. They all did. They raped women and mothers and wives and sisters."

"She's lucky to be alive," the elderly woman shouted.

I took a moment to relive all that had happened.

The Major ordered his soldiers, "Take these criminals away." His men led them into the jungle. Then he turned to Maman. "Are you okay, sister?"

"*Alhamdulillah*. Thank God," Maman replied. She was crying for joy.

"How did you find us?" I asked.

"The fisherman captain told us where you were."

"*Allahu Akbar, Alhamdulillah.*" I thanked God. It was a miracle.

As the Major took my hand and helped me onto the boat, the screams of the girls and women pleading for their lives reverberated in my head. Maman and Moise, my sisters and brother Raja followed. Then all the men and elders, women and boys and girls followed, until the boat was full.

Soon we heard gunshots in the distance.

"They are killing the rebels," a boy said.

"Leolina, wake up." Raja's voice woke me from a deep sleep. "We are back in Baraka."

I got off the boat and sat under a big tree which provided shade from the sun.

The next day Uncle Major returned and sat with all the rescued people from the boat. A goat was being barbecued, and someone was preparing a huge *fufu*.

"Come, let's eat something before you start your journey," the Major said. He walked with me to where everyone was eating barbecued goat meat, bananas and *fufu*. But I had lost my appetite. Maman packed a banana and a piece of meat for me to eat later.

"It's time to go," the Major said.

The same boat that we were on was at the dock and ready for boarding. After we embarked, the fisherman captain said, "Alright people, it's time to set out. Pray for a safe journey."

"Bye, Leolina," Uncle Major called. "Don't forget me."

"Adieu, Uncle Major," I called back. His soldiers escorted our boat until we were far out into the lake.

The sun set. It was dark all over the lake. I fell into a deep depression and would not talk to anyone. Nor was I hungry. I was tired of seeing children left orphaned because the war had taken their parents away and left them alone in the world. I felt like jumping overboard into the deep water.

But suddenly, as I sat teetering at the edge of the boat, a hand reached out and a voice said, "My dear. Are you here with me?"

"Humph!" I responded.

"I have been talking to you, but you are not

here. Where are you? Come sit near me." I held his hand, and gingerly moved away from the gunwale. "Be careful and don't worry. I won't let you fall."

Slowly I moved toward him, and he helped me sit down.

"Think about your maman, sisters and brothers. How could they live without you?"

I suddenly realized that if I had jumped into the darkness, the pain would not have ended there. It would have gone on to cause deep suffering to my loved ones.

"Please don't tell Maman what I was about to do. Thank you. May Allah bless you."

Then I went and sat next to Maman and my sisters and brothers.

In the morning, I didn't see the old man. I was looking around for him, when a boy asked, "Are you looking for someone?"

"Yes," I said. "Did you see a man sitting near me?"

"No, I didn't. Is he someone close to you?"

"Papa!" I blurted, and it started raining. Suddenly the sun shone through, and a rainbow arched across the lake.

Tanzania and the Refugee Camp

"We are in Tanzania now, and everyone has to get off."

The boat bumped against a deserted dock close to some mountains.

"What are we doing here in the middle of nowhere?" someone asked.

"I can't afford to lose my boat," the captain answered.

"Step off carefully, children. Hold each other's hands," Maman said. She was carrying Moise on her back.

I got off the boat first and led my sisters and brother to a safe spot on the shore.

We started climbing into the mountains along a steep and dangerous trail. We walked in file, one by one, and kept moving without looking over the cliff at the lake below. It started to pour.

"Maman, are you and Moise okay?" I shouted. "Fifi, Mimi, Raja, Massy—is everyone okay?"

We were soaked, but had to keep walking as we were still far from the nearest town, Rumonge.

Suddenly the storm intensified, causing the narrow path to become dangerously slippery. Maman slipped and fell, but landed on her knees. She fought to keep from falling flat as she was carrying my baby brother on her back.

"Maman!" we all screamed.

Fifi also slipped. She narrowly missed tumbling into the lake, but I held her hand tight. "It's okay, Fifi, don't look down. I've got you!"

The wind died down, but not the rain.

"Hold each other tight!" Maman shouted.

We were wet and frozen, and our spirits began to lag.

Mimi stopped. "I can't walk anymore."

Fifi said, "I can't feel my feet or my body anymore." She was trembling from the cold.

"Try to keep walking," Maman said.

"Give me your hand, Mimi." I said, reaching for her hand.

We struggled on, hoping it would lead us to safety. Luckily, the trail began to turn downward and the rain stopped.

As the sun set, I spotted some houses along the shore, and we made our way toward them. United Nations people and cars were waiting there with a big open truck. A UN worker gave us blankets, and we wrapped ourselves in them. Then we were helped into the truck. We drove past houses, and into the forest, until we reached a refugee camp.

A Tanzanian UN official greeted us in Swahili, and ushered us into a big open tent. "You will stay here until we find you a more permanent place."

Other aid workers gave us cookies and bottles of water. There was no place to sleep, so we just sat on the ground. "Eat and you will feel better. We'll be back tomorrow."

"Ah ah ah!" Maman fainted.

"Maman!" Fifi screamed.

"Please help!" I screamed.

"Move aside," said a man in Swahili. "I am a doctor." He helped Maman up.

"Maman will be okay, everything will be okay," I said to my brothers and sisters.

"Help me lead her out," a man called from outside the tent. The doctor and another man took Maman to the camp clinic.

An hour later, the doctor came back.

"Doctor!" I ran to him.

"She will be fine. She was suffering from exhaustion," he said. "She just needs rest."

"Are you sure?"

"Yes, she will be fine," the doctor said. "You can see her in the morning,"

A boy was standing next to him. "Hi," he said, "what's your name?"

"Leolina. What's yours?"

"Oz," he answered holding out his hand.

"That's my dad," he said, pointing to the doctor, who by now had stepped out of the tent.

A white woman rushed into the medical tent and stood, fuming, in front of the boy. "Oz, where have you been?" she asked in French. "I have been looking everywhere for you."

"I was visiting with Papa, Maman," he replied.

"Stay here, Oz," she said, angrily. "Don't run off." Then she followed her husband, the doctor, out into the rain.

Oz started talking in French in a jumble of words. "We've been here three days, but we are moving to the UNHCR protection camp near Kibondo. The UN and the Red Cross have contacted my grandpa in Belgium to get the right kind of visa for us to go there. It's complicated because my dad's Congolese."

"I hope things work out for you," I said, a bit sad to lose a potential friend.

Oz carried on with his story about who his parents were. "Maman is Congolese too, really. She was born in the Congo, even though her parents are from Belgium."

"Were you living in Kinshasa?"

"No," Oz answered. "We were living in Burundi. My father had his own clinic there. We lost everything when the war began."

Oz kept on talking and talking, and I fell asleep to the drone of his voice.

"Leolina!" Maman woke me up.

"Maman!" I was so happy to see her. "Are you okay?"

"The doctor gave me medication. Don't worry."

UNHCR Refugee Camp

A week or so later, a UN truck brought us to a UNHCR protection camp in Tanzania near Kibondo, where we were greeted by a UN official who held out his hand, smiling. "Welcome, madame," he said in Swahili. "Welcome to Tanzania."

Oz stopped by. He and his mother and father had been sent there just before us. I was so happy to see him. We hugged.

Every night in the refugee camp, my family and I would sit together in our mud hut with my friend Oz, who looked out for me. Though he was slim, his fierce eyes and wild hairdo scared off anyone who might threaten me. We were grateful to have one another, and I enjoyed laughing at his every joke.

Because of the mounds of clay inside our hut, we had to be careful when moving around. One night, after we finished saying our prayers, I took our little cooking oil lamp, which I'd made from a metal cup, cut a piece of cotton fabric, drenched it with oil, and lit it. It projected a small circle of light on the mud walls.

I picked up the lamp, but lost my balance and fell.

"Careful, Leolina," Maman said.

As I tried to stand up, Oz reached out. "Careful! Here, hold my hand," he said, helping me stand.

I stumbled into the small bedroom that I shared with my younger sister, Mimi, checking to make sure no dangerous snakes or insects were hiding in the crevices in the walls and ceiling. A chill went through my body. My hair stood on end, and a voice inside my head warned me to look up. I held my breath. A green mamba snake was hanging down above my head. I looked into its flaming red eyes. Its venomous tongue was flicking in and out, close to my face.

I recited, "Please Allah help me." Very slowly

and carefully, I started to shift over and sit on the floor. The snake jumped at me, but missed, hitting the mud wall behind me.

I screamed. My friend Oz heard my call for help, and quickly jumped in with a long piece of wood and hit the snake, killing it. Then he scooped it up and tossed it outside.

"That was so close!"

That wasn't the end of those venomous guests. Later that night, lying next to my sister, I spotted another snake.

"Mimi, don't move," I whispered, as the big snake rolled over our bellies. Once more I silently prayed. All I could see in the dark were its two flashing red eyes, like tiny torches. I shivered.

I held my breath as the creature slithered to the edge of the bed and dropped to the floor. It slinked away through a crack in the mud wall. I stepped outside, and in the pale light of the moon, watched it slither off. Mimi stumbled out noisily behind me.

"Shii!" I warned her. "It might come back."

Forgiveness

I heard that Sabina, daughter of Yayabo, who had betrayed Papa, was in the camp. I told Maman and she said, "Remember, Leolina, be kind and always forgive, no matter how much we have been wronged."

One night, while my family and I were sound asleep, I heard someone calling for help. I thought I was dreaming. I stepped outside and a little hand grabbed mine. I jumped.

"Please help, help my mom." A little boy was tugging at me. "Please, come help my mom. She's having a baby."

I followed him to his shelter, and there was Sabina, with a big belly, crying out in pain. "Please help me."

I leaned over and touched her forehead. She was burning with fever.

"Get water," I ordered the boy.

He ran out and returned with a bucket of

water. I wet a cloth and placed it on Sabina's head. Then I rushed outside and called for help. But no one responded.

Together the boy and I managed to pull Sabina up.

"We'll take her to the clinic," I said.

Somehow, together, we managed to get her there.

At the clinic, a nurse examined her. "I can't find a pulse," she said.

I refused to believe her. "That can't be."

"I'm sorry. There's nothing we can do."

"Please call a doctor," I insisted.

I prayed silently. Soon a doctor touched my shoulder.

"The nurse says she's dead," I said, sobbing.

"Wait outside," he said.

Sabina's son and I stepped outside. The boy was crying, and I held him close. It seemed like hours had passed.

Finally, a nurse came out. "Come in," she said.

As soon as the doctor saw me, he smiled.

"She's revived, and the baby is fine. We're treating the mother for malaria."

My prayers had been answered.

Sabina called out to me. "I'm so sorry for what my mom did."

"Don't blame yourself," I said.

Sabina started to call me sister, and not long after that, Yayabo came to the camp, as she too had become a refugee.

One morning I met her at the water pump. She heard that I had saved her daughter's life. I could hear her lost soul asking me to forgive her. But I refused to acknowledge her presence.

"Leolina!"

I could see that she was suffering, but I hurt too much. I just turned and walked away.

The following day at the pump, she called out to me again, "Leolina, please forgive me. I was wrong."

I turned around. She was crying. I heard my father's voice. "Leolina, forgive her."

"Papa," I called out.

Just then my Maman stepped behind me and put her hand on my shoulder. "Yayabo has been waiting for your forgiveness."

"Yes, Maman. Papa taught me not to keep bitterness in my heart. To do that gives power to those who have wronged you."

I turned to Yayabo. "I forgive you."

Epilogue: Canada

Like other French-speaking refugees from the Congo, Rwanda and Burundi, Canada chose to bring our family to Quebec. We were hoping for peace in the Congo, so that we could go back home when it was safe, but that peace never came.

In the Congo, before the wars, in our home Maison Rouge, we had a blessed life. We were so happy. We went to school, and my father was planning to send me to Paris to study medicine, so that I could open my own clinic and serve our community in Uvira.

We are thankful that Canada took us out of the UNHCR camp, but life here has also been hard. Compared to the good times we had in the Congo before the wars—surrounded by friends and family—life here in Canada is lonely at times.

Author's Note

To my beautiful Maman, Lina Iza Leonie Chikwerere Biraheka Zubeda—Maman, your support has made me into the woman I am today. You taught me that being a girl and woman is a blessing to all humanity, and that love, kindness, support, and the power of women is the way to life and healing. May Allah bless you, my mother, and grant you health and long life, Ameen.

To my beloved Papa, Mzee Juma Omari, may Allah have mercy on your soul and may you rest in peace. Your inquisitive, logical mind, wisdom, beautiful soul and kind heart taught me to be a good human being; to empower girls and women through education and knowledge; to believe in myself, my mission, and destiny; to love and support others with love, peace and forgiveness, and to love and believe in Allah—our maker, supporter, and guardian.

To my loving family, my beautiful sisters Farida Juma, Shany Juma and Mwasiti Juma; my brothers Abdoul Dushimiyimana, Rajabu Juma, Moise Juma, Kizungu Eduard and Vay Kaba; my nephews, Amari Lwazi Juma, Lucas Zelaya, Ayaan Dushimiye, and my nieces, Aliya Leonie Juma and Ayaana Dushimiye; and my sister-in-law, Saidati Uwimana. To my dear relatives, Maman Chikwerere Chekanabo Godesia and Muraranya Estella; Uncle Muderwa Jean Chrisostome bin Nakamaga; Papa Sudi Ngabo Rajabu; Juma Idrisa, Aziza Nkundwanabashaka, Pili Sumaili, Maneno and Sikujuwa; Kaka Papu Menga and Wakilongo Wika Kubama. Rest in peace, Uncle Joache Muraranya, my brothers Guillaume Chimong Kaba and Sumaili Juma, and my sister Furaha Juma.

Many thanks to my dear Valerie Sara Price, Mr. Wilson

Price and Helene; mom Beverly Irene Hicks and William Temereski; Cyrille Avul Nzenza; Kaka Omari Musheshe; Adam Rajab and Jabil Mbilikira of Tanzania.

To my beloved sisters, mothers and grand-mothers all over the world. We have all faced and survived the same pain and tears, though our personal experiences may differ. Sisters, you are love and peace, life givers, educators, supporters and saviors. Never lose hope. Believe in the strong heart and peaceful spirit that Almighty God, your source, has created. Connect to your Creator, as I have with Allah, my guardian God. Experience His strength, protection, blessing, love, peace and light. Bless and support others as you gain experience, knowledge and wisdom. Stand tall, love, bless and be kind to yourself. Life is a journey with many lessons to learn every day. Have faith, and honor and love your parents. Learn especially from your mothers, your first loves, educators, guides and nurturers.

I am blessed that, with my friend and colleague, Myungsook Lee, we have been able to support women and girls in their recovery, giving them hope, self-belief and trust.

To my dear friend, Norma J Hill, thank you for supporting and believing in me, reminding me of who I am, seeing the gifted and talented story teller and the creative and unique artist in me.

Special thanks to Michael Katz and Carol Frank for believing in me. And I appreciate the support given by Tradewind Books.

Heartfelt appreciation to you, all my family and friends in Canada, in Africa and around the world. May Allah bless you, and much love to you and your loved ones.